MY SISTER IS ANNOYING!
and other prayers for children

By Fr. Joe Kempf
with BIG AL

Illustrated by Chris Sharp

Liguori
ONE LIGUORI DRIVE
LIGUORI MO 63057-9999
314.464.2500

This book belongs to Abigail Frenzel

This book belongs to: Abigail Frenzel

Imprimi Potest:
Thomas D. Picton, C.Ss.R.
Provincial, Denver Province
The Redemptorists

Published by Liguori Publications
Liguori, Missouri 63057, USA
To order, call 800-325-9521.
www.liguori.org

ISBN 978-0-7648-1827-1

Liguori Publications, a nonprofit corporation, is an apostolate of the Redemptorists. To learn more about the Redemptorists, visit Redemptorists.com.

Printed and assembled in Mexico
13 12 11 10 09   5 4 3 2 1
First edition

Acknowledgement

To You, Oh God, I offer this,
with thanks—and with a prayer,
that all who ever touch this book
will know how much You care.

So many are a part of it,
I could not thank them here.
So I pray that You will bless them,
and always hold them near.

Whatever age the reader,
where'er their life has led,
through what they find inside this book,
by You may they be fed.

—Fr. Joe Kempf

Prayers in This Book

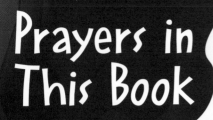

Hello!

Introduction

If there is a child in your life, yours is a beautiful and holy calling; for God will love that child through you.

Your call is also difficult, for you will always be letting go. In that, you understand something at the heart of God.

The prayers in this book are for the children entrusted to your care...and also for you.

May your children find God through you. May you see the world anew through their eyes. And through it all, may you be able to trust that you are never alone.

In Jesus,
Father Joe

My Sister Is Annoying

My sister is annoying, God.
She might not try to be.
Though family is important,
it's also hard for me.

I do not always like her.
Yet, You live in her heart.
Deep down I love my sister.
Let this be a new start.

Family
is hard
sometimes.

I Put Myself Into Your Hands

I put myself into Your hands,
to start this brand new day.
I'll do my best to love and share.
I'll try to live Your way.

Because You are so wonderful,
I pray to be like You.
Your love means so much to me.
I love You, God, I do.

It's a
new day!

When There's Time to Be Outside

When there's time to be outside,
in rain or snow or sun,
it's good to smell, to touch, to hear,
to see what You have done.

You love this world You made, oh God.
It's holy, good, and true.
You count on us to love it well,
'cause this world's filled with You.

When No One Picks Me for Their Team

When no one picks me for their team,
dear Jesus, I feel sad.
Maybe I'm not strong or fast.
That doesn't make me bad.

They think I have no value.
On their team, I won't start.
But to You, oh God, I'm special.
You hold me in Your heart.

Sad to feel left out.

I'm Lucky to Have Food Today

I'm lucky to have food today.
They say I should be glad,
but this is not my favorite food.
I'd say it tastes quite bad.

Mom said people starve each day,
and we all need to share.
Help me to remember them,
and fill my heart with care.

There's a Baby in Our House

There's a baby in our house,
and everyone is glad.
Mostly I am happy,
but sometimes I am sad.

My mom is tired and busy,
yet she says I'm special, too.
I guess that's what Your heart is like.
You love us all, You do!

Giggle

So Many Things Are Changing

So many things are changing.
The world is different now.
I'm told that I will be okay,
but I just can't see how.

Help me to be brave, oh God,
when what I feel is scared.
Help me trust that You will help,
that love is always there.

I know that You are with me.
You'll never go away.
Things aren't the way I wanted,
but You are here to stay.

You are always here.

I'm Feeling Kind of Sick Today

I'm feeling kind of sick today.
It really isn't fun.
There isn't much that I can do.
I wish that this was done.

I pray for all who hurt today.
It's one thing I can do.
And some day I'll feel better,
'cause You make all things new.

I'll feel better.

I'm Glad I Have a Grandpa

I'm glad I have a grandpa.
I love to hear him talk.
My grandpa says he knew me
when I could not yet walk!

Please take good care of Grandpa, God.
He's old, but also wise.
He teaches me to see the world
with loving, holy eyes.

Thank
You for
Grandpa!

Today It Is My Birthday

Today it is my birthday.
I'm glad I came to be!
It is so great to be alive.
Thank You for making me.

You know that I'm not perfect,
but I am good, it's true.
I am the child of Mom and Dad,
and I'm the child of You!

It's my
Birthday!

They Pick on Him
at School Sometimes

They pick on him at school sometimes.
Some people call him names.
They say, "Hey, we don't like you,"
and "You can't play our games."

It must make You so sad, dear God,
when we are so unkind.
At times like that, we just don't see.
We then are truly blind.

For You love every single child.
We each belong to You.
Help me reach out to those who hurt.
I want to be like You.

Help us to be kind.

I Miss My Dog

I miss my dog. He died, You know.
Now things just aren't the same.
We used to hike and run around
and play all kinds of games.

Even though I miss him here
(the house seems quiet now),
I hope he's truly happy,
that he's with You somehow.

Do You Worry About My Family?

Do You worry about my family?
You know, dear God, I do.
When things are hard and scary,
I don't know what to do.

Please, dear Jesus, help me see
that in my home, You dwell.
Help me love my family.
Please help me love them well.

Sometimes things are scary.

You Know Why I Am Angry, God

You know why I am angry, God.
It's hard when life's not fair.
To hurt them back won't help at all,
and so I say this prayer.

You ask me to forgive them,
as You've forgiven me.
I'll need Your help to do that.
Dear Jesus, please help me.

Help me to
forgive.

How Could I Thank You, Father?

How could I thank You, Father,
for all of Your great love?
Your blessings all around me,
below me and above.

You love me more than I can know
in ways I'll never see.
Please know that I am grateful now,
and I will always be.

My Grandma Died

My grandma died; I'll miss her so.

Dear Jesus, please help me.

Please let her know that I still care.

Give her a hug for me.

You must be glad to see her,

though I'm sad we're apart.

Tell her I'll always love her

and keep her in my heart.

I'm sad about Grandma.

For Now, I'll Just Be Quiet

For now, I'll just be quiet.

I have no words to say.

Yet even when I speak no words,

You hear me when I pray.

When my words just don't seem right,

I trust that You still hear.

We'll sit here in the silence

and still be very near.

I'll just be quiet.

When I Look Back Upon This Day

When I look back upon this day,
I see how much You care,
blessing me in countless ways,
and so I say this prayer.

I thank You, Jesus, for my life,
for family and for friends.
I thank You, Jesus, most of all,
for love that never ends.

How blessed I am!

Mom Said I
Should Go
to Bed

Mom said I should go to bed,
but I am kind of scared.
The dark can feel so lonely, God.
Please help me know You're there.

Watch over me and keep me safe.
Keep scary thoughts away.
Help me think of happy things
and know You're here, I pray.

Now It's Time to Fall Asleep

Now it's time to fall asleep,
for peaceful dreams and rest.
I put my day into Your hands,
since You know what is best.

All those I love, I give to You.
I even give You me.
And when tomorrow comes once more,
how blessed again I'll be!

Peaceful
dreams.

CD TRACK LISTING

Track 01: My Sister Is Annoying
Track 02: I Put Myself Into Your Hands
Track 03: When There's Time to Be Outside
Track 04: When No One Picks Me for Their Team
Track 05: I'm Lucky to Have Food Today
Track 06: There's a Baby in Our House
Track 07: So Many Things Are Changing
Track 08: I'm Feeling Kind of Sick Today
Track 09: I'm Glad I Have a Grandpa
Track 10: Today It Is My Birthday
Track 11: They Pick on Him at School Sometimes
Track 12: I Miss My Dog
Track 13: Do You Worry About My Family?
Track 14: You Know Why I Am Angry, God
Track 15: How Could I Thank You, Father?
Track 16: My Grandma Died
Track 17: For Now, I'll Just Be Quiet
Track 18: When I Look Back Upon This Day
Track 19: Mom Said I Should Go to Bed
Track 20: Now It's Time to Fall Asleep

©&℗ 2009 Fr. Joe Kempf • BIG AL™ Fr. Joe Kempf
Running Time: 23:56